CONTENTS

TOWPATH FISHERMEN, 2004

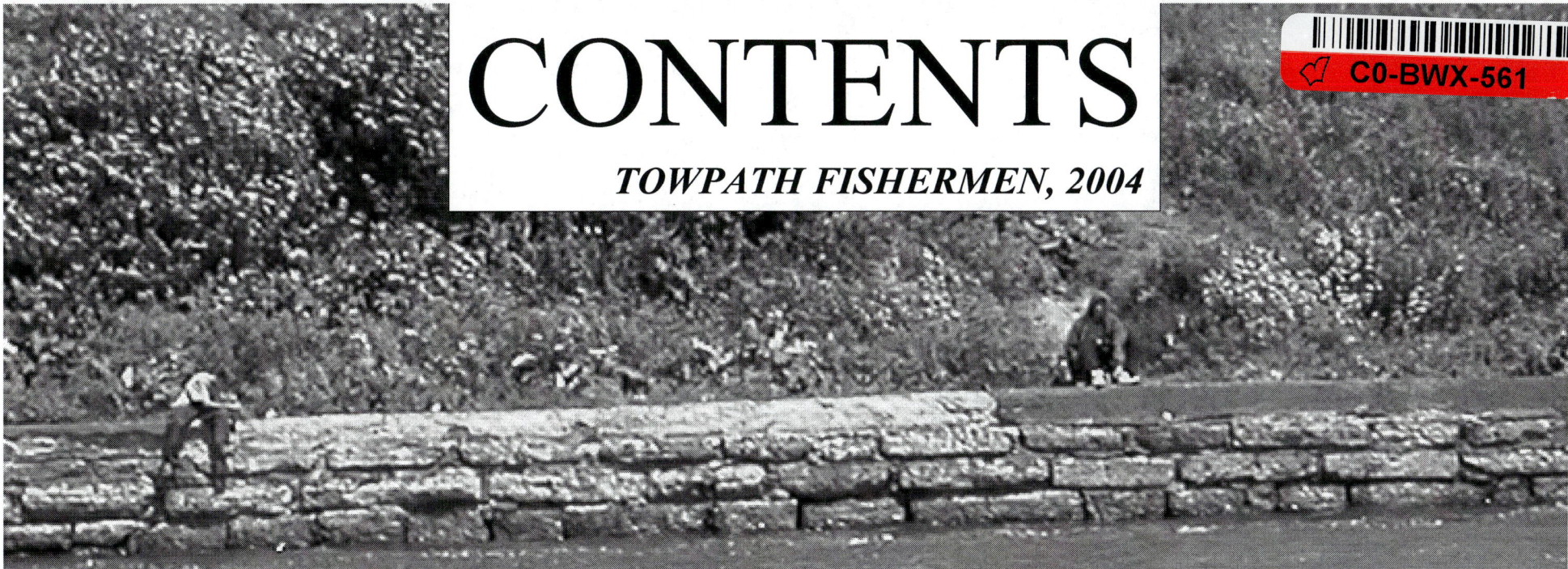

Canals in the North East, 1860

America was jealous of Buffalo and it showed. Note the names of the westernmost canals….(Wabash and *Erie*, Miami and *Erie* and Ohio and *Erie*). They all followed the original Erie; only the Champlain had an earlier completion date (1823), but even by then, most of the Erie Canal (completed 1825) was in use.

All of the canals shown had their own slips, locks and basins, so the subject of North American canals is more extensive than you might first think. There is something very ironic about this map. Note the Welland Canal, a predecessor of the St. Lawrence Seaway system. The tiny Canadian canal would one day help beat the mighty Erie at its own game. The Port Colborne locks are less than an hour from Buffalo.

1860 American Canal Map, from Brinkley, Alan. *American History A Survey,* McGraw-Hill, 1995. Reproduced with permission of the McGraw-Hill Companies.

3

Black River Canal

Champlain Canal (1823)

Oswego Canal (1828)

Lake Ontario

Rochester

Oswego

Rome

Erie Canal (1825)

Troy

Welland Canal (1833)

Buffalo

Syracuse

Utica

Albany

Genessee Valley Canal

Chenango Canal (1837)

NEW YORK

Olean

Binghamton

Hudson R.

Lake Erie

Cleveland

PENNSYLVANIA

Miami and Erie Canal (1845)

Wabash and Erie Canal (1856)

OHIO

Ohio and Erie Canal (1832)

Wheeling

Columbus

Pennsylvania Canal (1840)

Rail link

Delaware and Raritan Canal (1834)

New York

New Brunswick

ILLINOIS

INDIANA

Pittsburgh

C.&O. Canal

Johnstown

Hollidaysburg

Harrisburg

Trenton

Columbia

Philadelphia N.J.

Terre Haute

Cincinnati

Marietta

Baltimore

St. Louis

Wabash R.

Ohio R.

Evansville

Louisville

Portsmouth

Cumberland

MD.

Chesapeake and Ohio Canal (1850)

Washington, D.C.

DEL.

VIRGINIA

Mississippi R.

Chesapeake Bay

0	150 Miles	
0	150 Kilometers	

Canals

Rail link

(1833) Date completed

New York State's Canal System Prior To 1918

The name change - from *Erie Canal* to *Barge Canal* - came from the New York State Barge Canal Act of 1903 - (though N.Y.S. began calling it the Erie Barge Canal in the 1990s). Most (not all!) of the Erie, together with the Champlain, Oswego and Cayuga/Seneca would become the State Barge Canal System. The Black River canal (from Rome north to Ogdensburg) , and the Buffalo to Tonawanda section of the Erie Canal would be abandoned in 1917. The new system would not include towpaths.

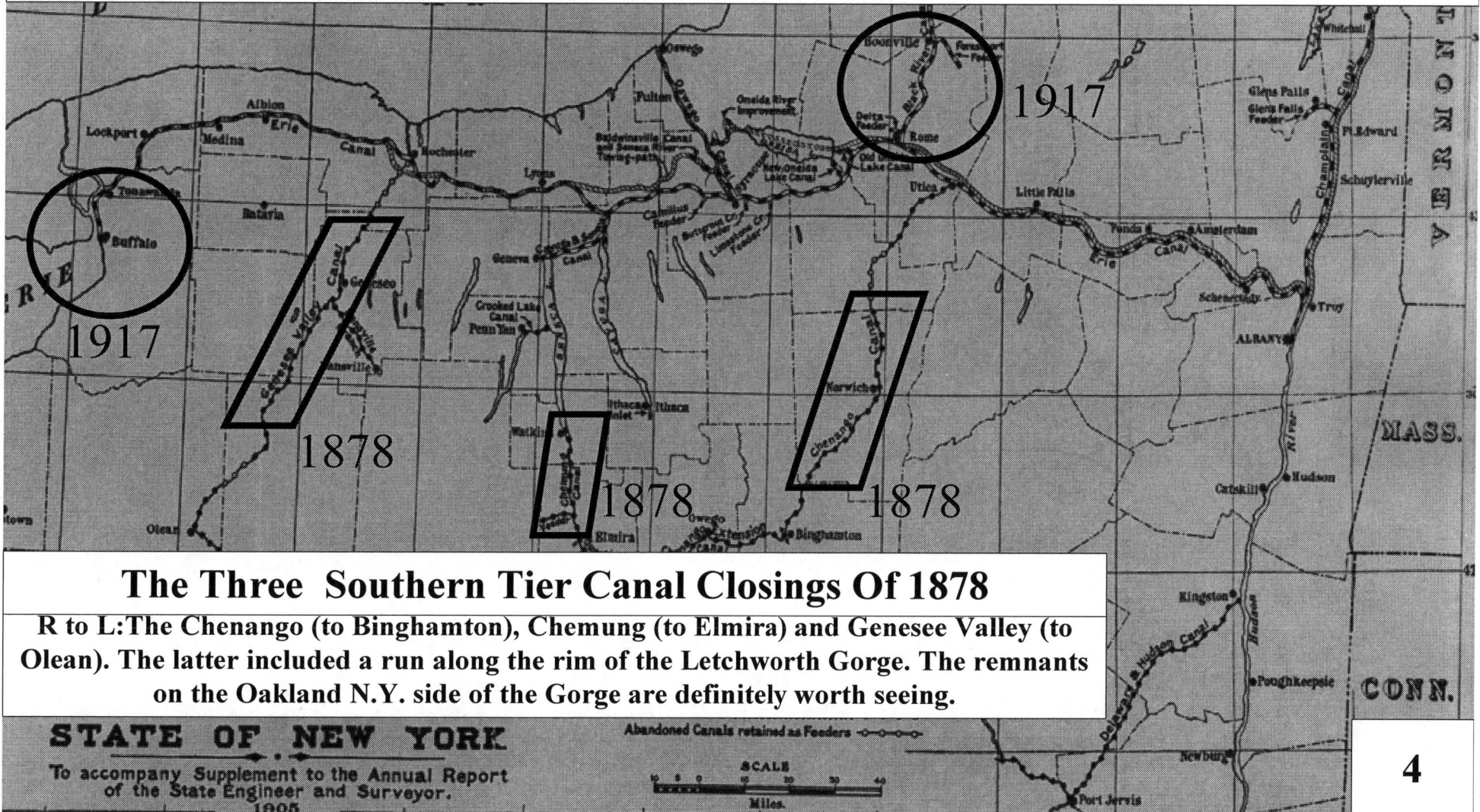

The Three Southern Tier Canal Closings Of 1878

R to L:The Chenango (to Binghamton), Chemung (to Elmira) and Genesee Valley (to Olean). The latter included a run along the rim of the Letchworth Gorge. The remnants on the Oakland N.Y. side of the Gorge are definitely worth seeing.

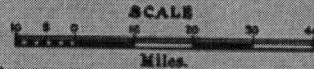

Erie Canal locks between Austin and Hamilton Streets *c. 1900*

1924 Niagara Street, with its mansard hip roof, and the brick bi-level 1920 Niagara Street. Even with the latter's penthouse, both are unmistakable. The 2004 view is from near the I-190's Austin Street exit ramp.

Erie Canal Towpath Site, near Amherst Street

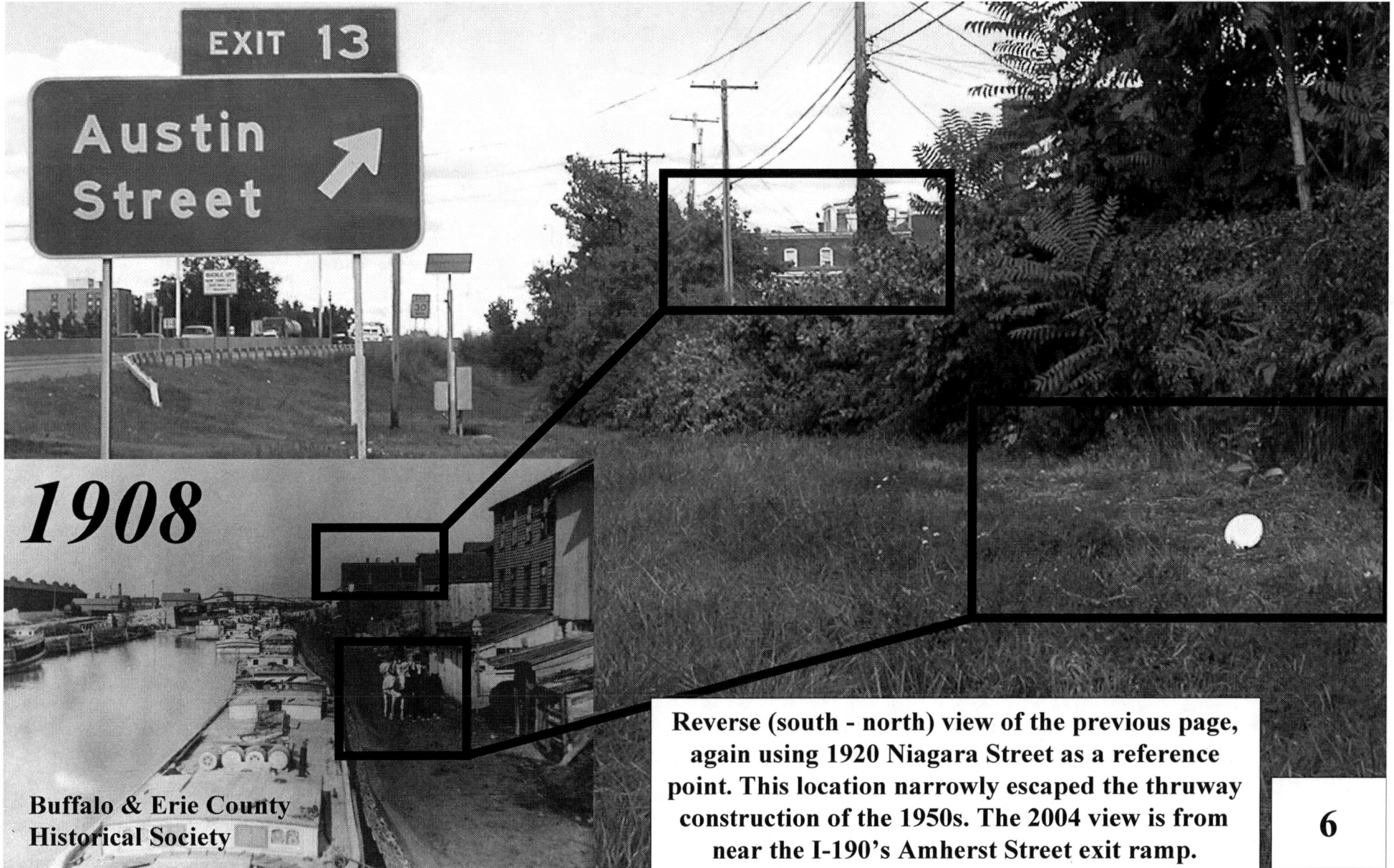

EXIT 13

Austin Street ↗

1908

Buffalo & Erie County Historical Society

Reverse (south - north) view of the previous page, again using 1920 Niagara Street as a reference point. This location narrowly escaped the thruway construction of the 1950s. The 2004 view is from near the I-190's Amherst Street exit ramp.

6

Black Rock Canal

The northern point of the city of Buffalo's remaining canal system. In the background, a pivoted section of the 1873 International Railroad Bridge opens in unison with the gates of the 1906 Black Rock ship lock. A mile to the south, under the Ferry Street bascule bridge, is a fragile piece of Erie Canal towpath.

Both pictures taken from the *Miss Buffalo*, August 2004

Black Rock Channel

The Erie Canal originally re-entered the mainland immediately north of the rail bridge. The east/city side carried the towpath of the Erie Canal; at this point, the canal utilized the Black Rock *Channel*. The west/Squaw Island side was known both as the Black Rock *Harbor* (below left) and the Black Rock Canal. The former was an echo of the 1820s dispute between Buffalo and Black Rock over the Erie Canal's western terminus. The major difference between this section of the Erie Canal and the inland parts is that the Thruway parallels rather than replaces it, so a lot of stonework survives. The area is remarkable for its massive engineering works.

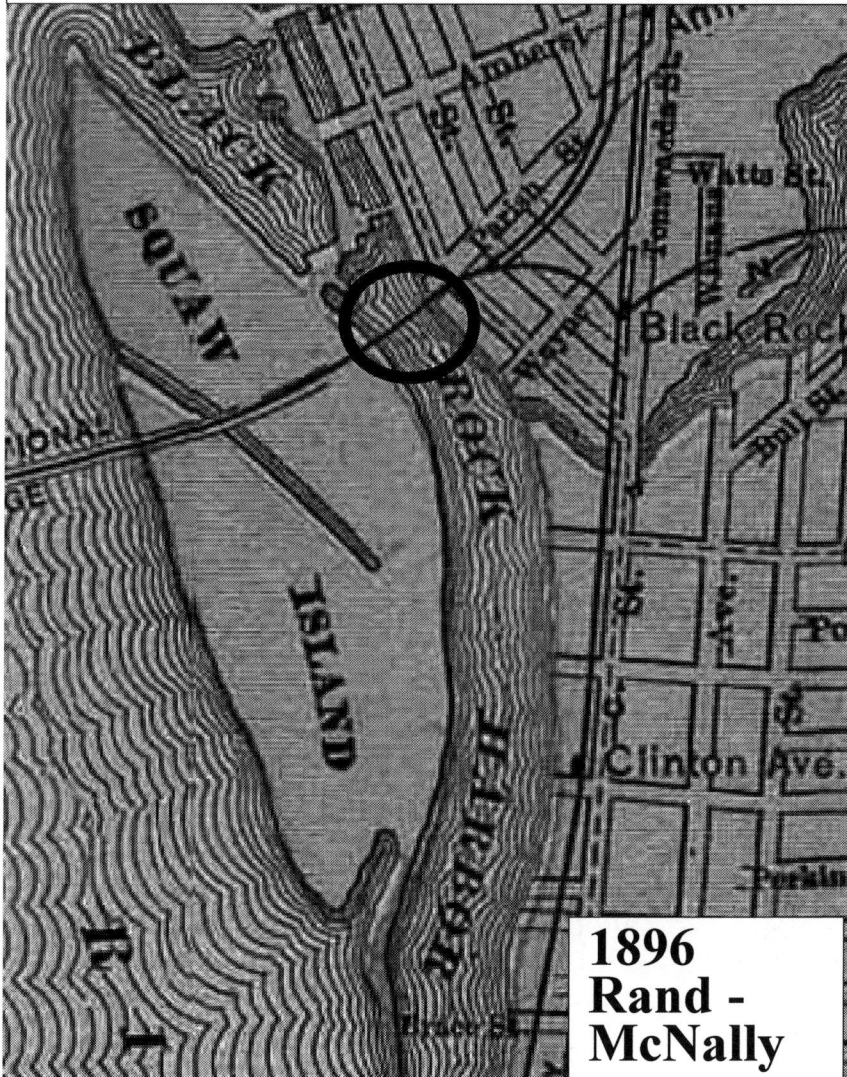

1896 Rand - McNally

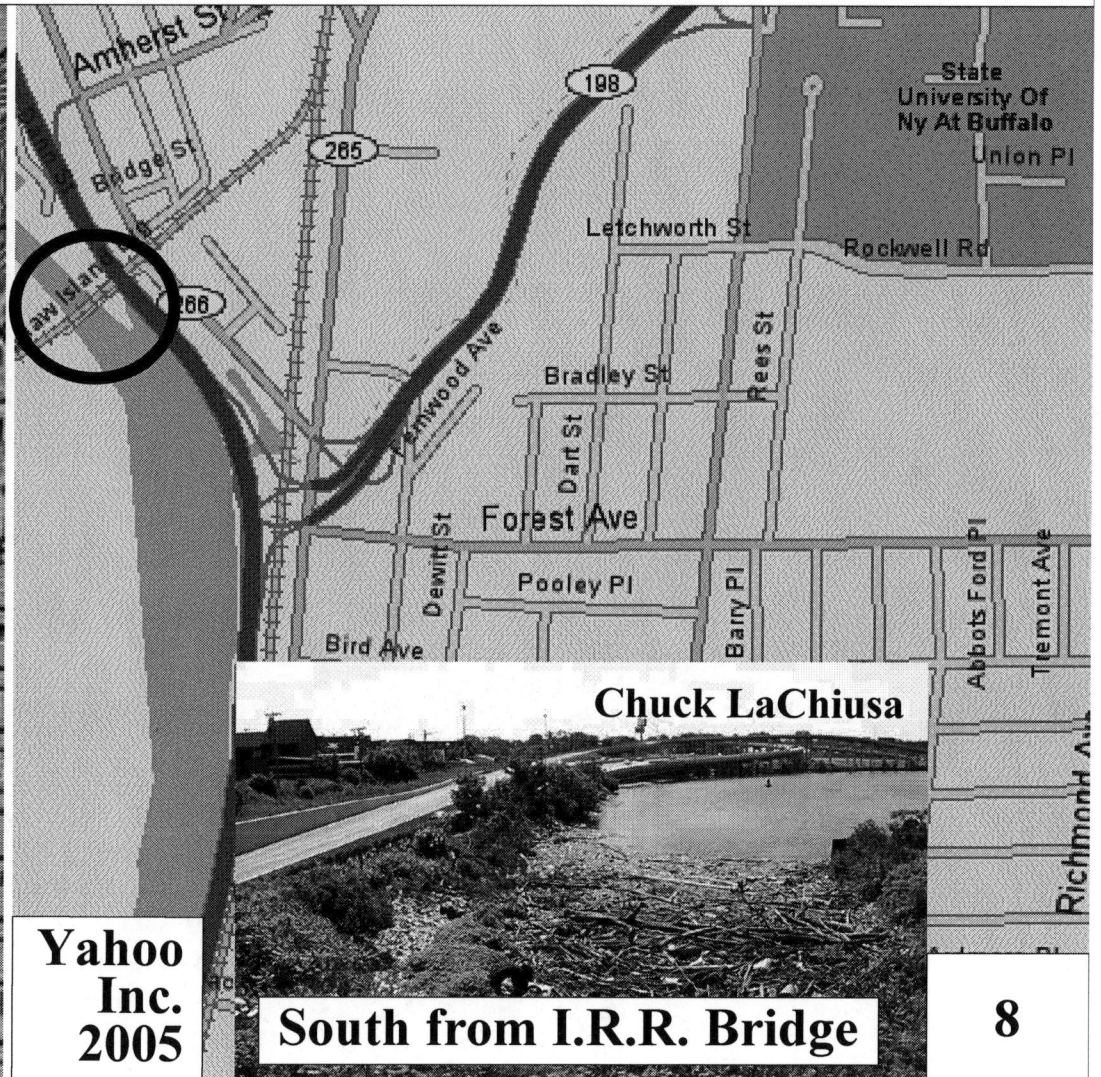

Yahoo Inc. 2005

Chuck LaChiusa

South from I.R.R. Bridge

8

Scajaquada Creek

The map at lower right shows how the creek was reshaped for thruway construction in the 1950s, by-passing the original mouth (main photo) and giving it the deceptive appearance of a slip. The creek was used by barges to a "short distance past Niagara St" (Richard Garrity in *Canal Boatman),* and so was part of the Erie system even though not a canal. Signs such as the *Old Navy Yard* one (at Niagara and Forest Streets, close to the creek and expressway), are all too rare in Buffalo.

NEW YORK

OLD NAVY YARD
1813
FIVE VESSELS OF COMMODORE
PERRY'S FLEET WERE RECONDITIONED
ON SOUTH BANK AT MOUTH OF
NEARBY SCAJAQUADA CREEK

STATE EDUCATION
DEPARTMENT 1956

9

Foot of Massachusetts Avenue

1889

Buffalo & Erie County Historical Society

Water → Intake

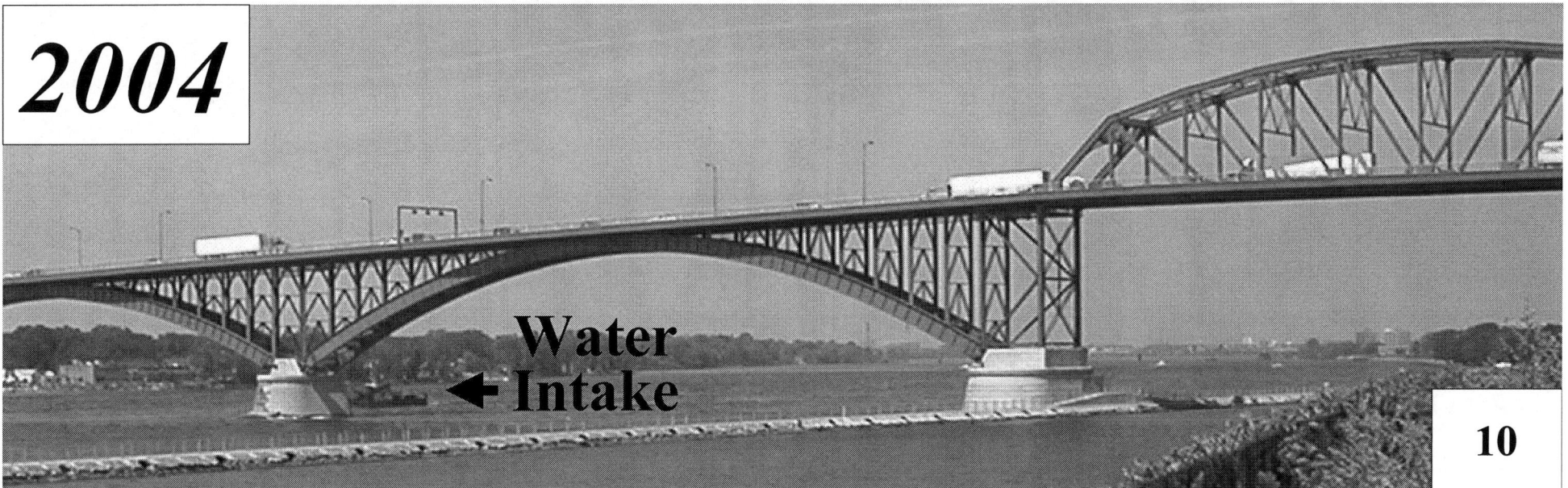

2004

Water → Intake

10

Both pictures show the IRR bridge in the background, the old water intake station and the Bird Island Pier/Black Rock Harbor Wall. Note (1) the wall dividing the Black Rock Channel (of the Erie Canal) and the Black Rock Harbor, and (2) the mule team at lower left, both in the 1889 photograph. The Peace Bridge dates from 1927. Viewed from the Riverwalk.

Mouth of the Downtown Section

1896 Rand McNally

Towpath Remains

Moving south, we see the mouth of the downtown Erie Canal, abandoned with the other Niagara sections in 1917. The Rowing Club's dock now sits in the middle of the mouth. The wall between Erie Canal (Black Rock Channel) and Black Rock Harbor was removed in 1905. This important site is clearly visible from the Bird Island Pier, the Riverwalk, and of course from the water.

Mouth of the Downtown Section
in 1889

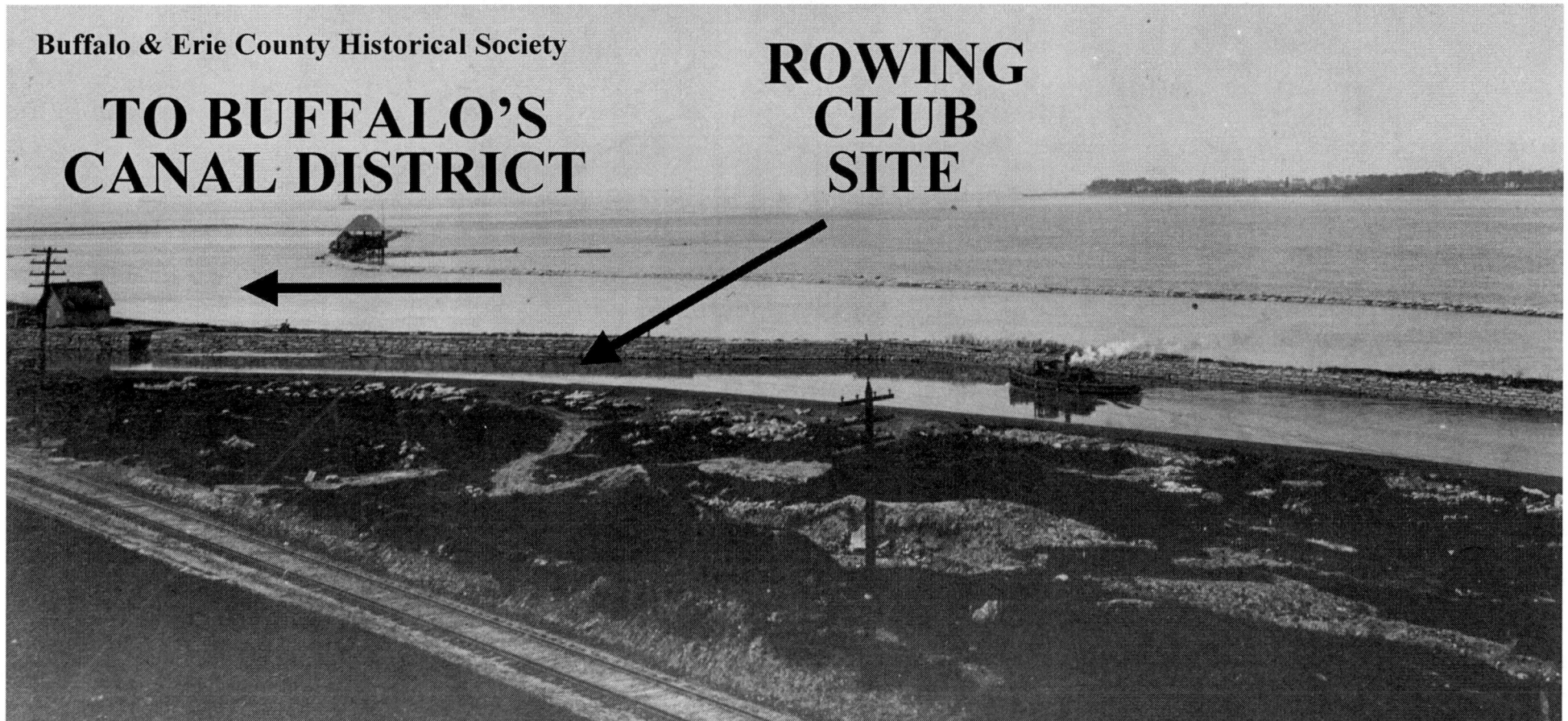

Buffalo & Erie County Historical Society

TO BUFFALO'S CANAL DISTRICT

ROWING CLUB SITE

Another view of the site on the last page. The Erie Canal continued toward Buffalo's lower downtown, while the stone point continued north as the dividing wall.The towpath (bank nearest camera) remained in regular recreational use until the Thruway sealed it off in the late 1950's. The few fishermen who still use it in 2004 speak highly of it. Next, a look at Rome, N.Y. - remember this is the same canal and the same towpath.

12

ERIE CANAL
CONSTRUCTION BEGAN HERE
JULY 4, 1817. FIRST BOAT
TRIP FROM ROME TO UTICA
OCT. 22, 1819. 363 MILE
CANAL COMPLETED OCT. 20, 1825

A comparison with the (same!) towpath and canal at the Rome, N.Y. Erie Canal Village. Mules and horses give rides on a replica packet, or passenger, barge. This is the enlarged 1835 (2nd) version of the Erie Canal, though there are remains of the original ditch on the museum grounds. Note the towpath change bridge with its double ramps (lower left). A similar bridge was located at the foot of Jersey Street in Buffalo. Also - the Fort Bull massacre site (1756) is on the grounds, and Fort Stanwix is two miles away.

13

Porter Avenue Bridge

The gracious arch and the Buffalo section of the Erie Canal are long gone, but the west abutment is unchanged from this *c.* 1930 view. The eastern one survives minus its columns. The canal had been officially abandoned in 1917. Below: the site in 2004.

Erie Basin *in 1884*   # Erie Basin Marina *in 2001*

The Erie Basin *Marina* dates from the 1970s, but the original Erie Basin was dug in the 1850s. Its once prominent slips are now anonymous stubs, and vague condominium names tell nothing of the area's bustling history. A look at the 1884 map helps correct this. The area was so busy that another canal - the 1830s Evans Ship Canal - ran from the river to half-way between the Peacock and Erie slips. The Evans Slip survived near the Marine Drive Apartments until the 1970s. At the remaining mouth of the Coit Slip a new (2005) restaurant has opened. We may know the spot as the Shanghai Red's site, but a close look at the bottom right of the 1884 map shows the words *Freight Shed*.

ERIE

PEACOCK

COIT

15

In 1850 Evans Slip In 1959

Western New York Heritage

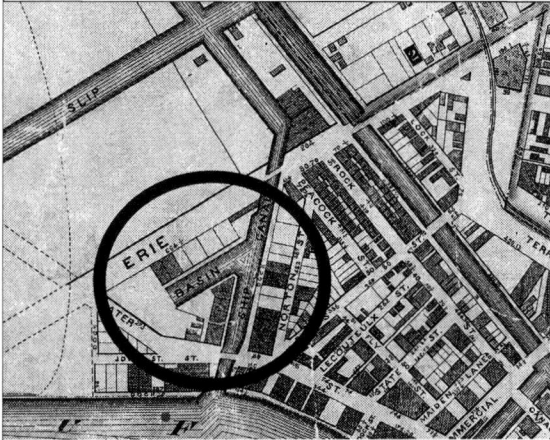

Buffalo & Erie
County Historical
Society

CANAL STREET SITE

The Y shape formed by the mouth of the Evans Ship Canal and its basin was as clear in 1959 as in 1850. The Coit Slip is visible to the left of the photograph; in 1850 it had yet to be dug. Canal Street had been renamed Dante Place in 1909; in 1850 it was still Rock Street. In 1959 the Marine Drive Apartments were still the Dante Place Projects. The Western New York Vietnam Veterans Memorial now occupies the filled (in 1974) mouth of the Evans Slip. 47 Marine Drive (front left apartment building) occupies the site of the Evans Elevator.

16

Main - Hamburg Canal - Abandoned *(1901)*

The Main-Hamburg appears to have been filled in increments, as and when the land was needed. Twenty two years after this picture was taken, Mayor Frank X. Schwab's 1923 report to the Common Council included a reference to *"the abatement of the Hamburg Canal nuisance"*. We can see that barges were abandoned there, then probably damaged by construction of the Hamburg Drain and Thruway. There still could be remnants in the filled bed.

17

Main-Hamburg Canal Bed

Western New York Heritage

As with the Porter Avenue bridge, the 19th century stonework was re-used in successive Louisiana Street bridges. The mile-long Main Hamburg formed a rough 'T' (see back cover) with the Commercial Slip and the main Erie Canal. As such it was, with the Ohio Basin and the Republic St. slip, one of the farthest western points ever reached by the waterway system. But by all accounts, (literally!), the filled bed with its pleasant foliage is a great improvement. As the hydraulic system had fallen into disuse, less flow entered the MH, turning it into a virtual cesspool. The I-190 manages to parallel, partially occupy, then straddle the bed. This view is from near Scott Street, with the bed continuing right/south to Hamburg Street. There the MH and Hydraulic canals met, and there the storm sewer pumping station is now located (*important*).

18

Commercial Slip

Discharge end - the Hamburg Drain sits squarely in the middle of the Commercial Slip, following the canal routes. This is a major obstacle to the Erie Canal Harbor project.

The Prime Slip was located two blocks from here (see cover). The observation deck behind Memorial Auditorium overlooks this, the original (1825) western terminus of the Erie Canal.

Clark and Skinner Canal Mouth

1863 Bird's Eye View, photographed at BECHS by Chuck LaChiusa

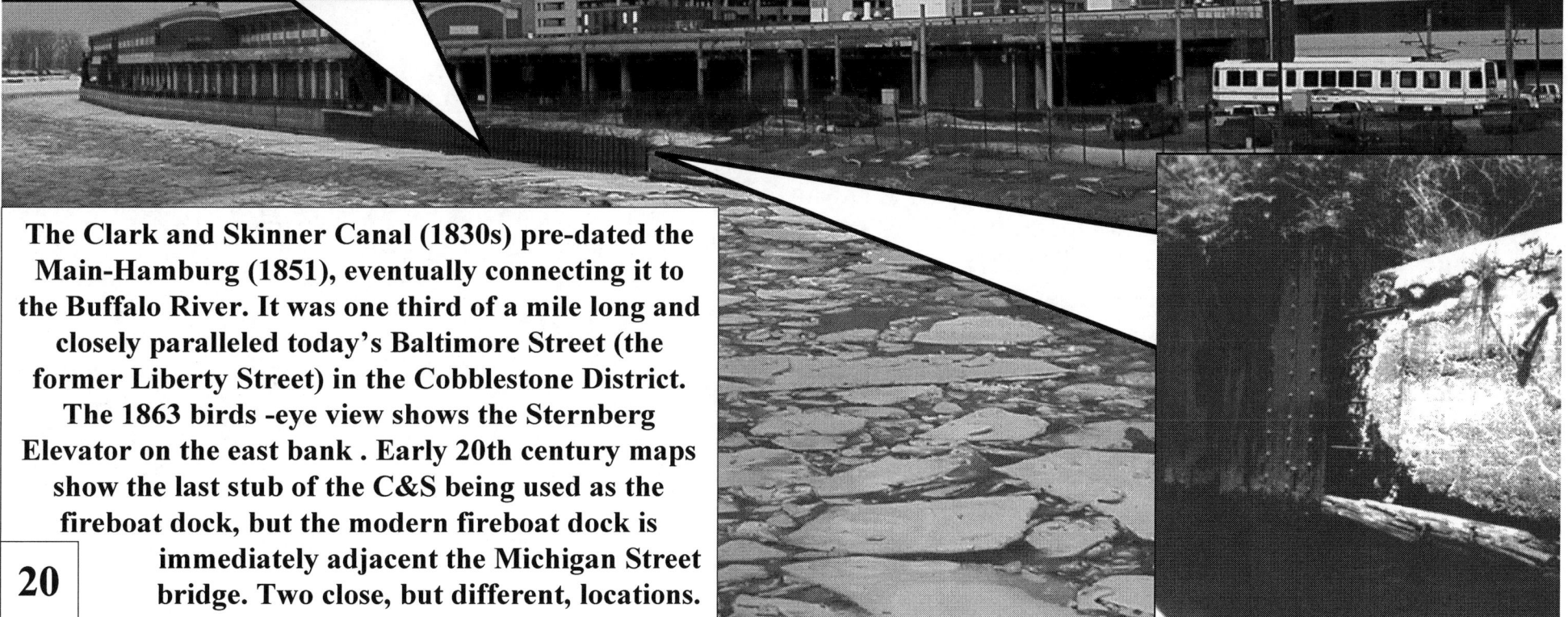

The Clark and Skinner Canal (1830s) pre-dated the Main-Hamburg (1851), eventually connecting it to the Buffalo River. It was one third of a mile long and closely paralleled today's Baltimore Street (the former Liberty Street) in the Cobblestone District. The 1863 birds -eye view shows the Sternberg Elevator on the east bank . Early 20th century maps show the last stub of the C&S being used as the fireboat dock, but the modern fireboat dock is immediately adjacent the Michigan Street bridge. Two close, but different, locations.

Clark and Skinner Canal Site

From South Park Avenue near Columbia Street, in the Cobblestone District. Unfortunately the sidewalk plaque disappeared in 2004. The 1904 photograph shows squatter's boats after the canal had been abandoned (in 1901). Such boats were one form of the low-income housing of the day. You can still see the tell-tale cluster of manhole covers at former bridge-over-canal, now street-over-sewer locations.

1904 photo foreground: Jewett Foundry.
Background: Schoellkopf Tannery and Perry Street bridge.

"East Bank of Clark & Skinner Canal"

21

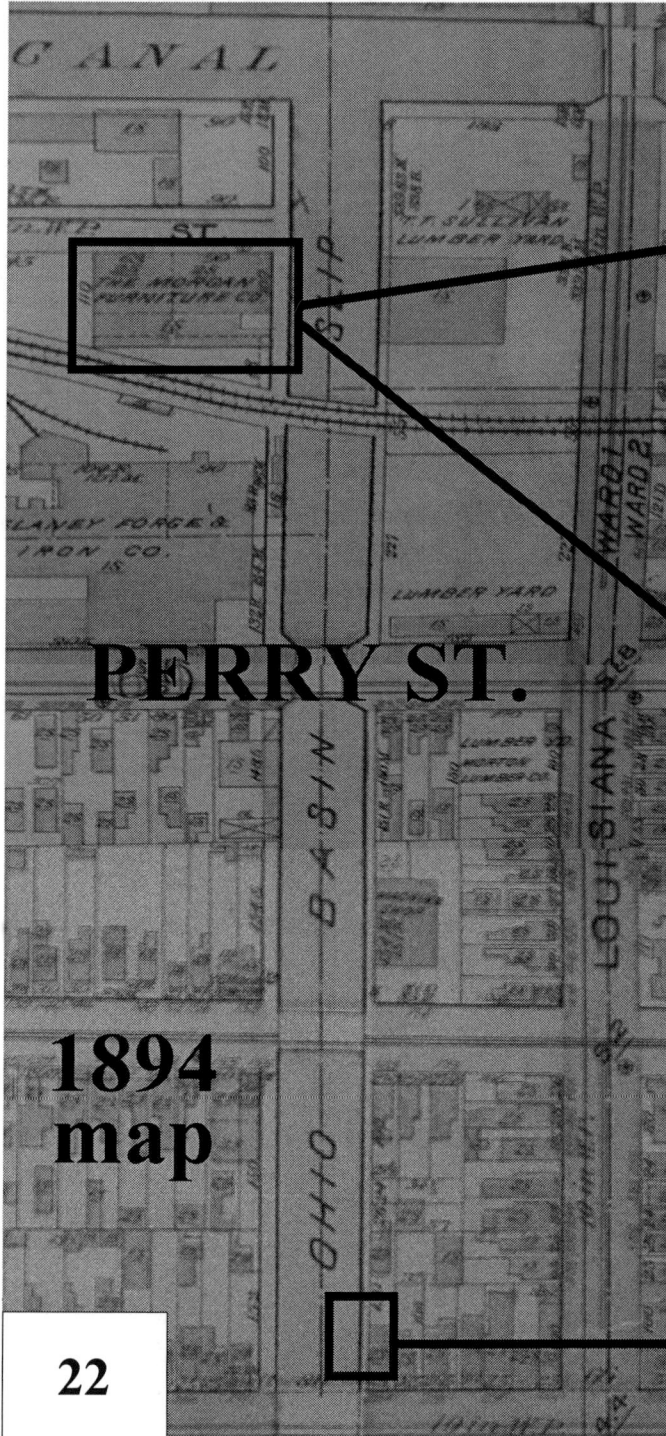

PERRY ST.

1894 map

22

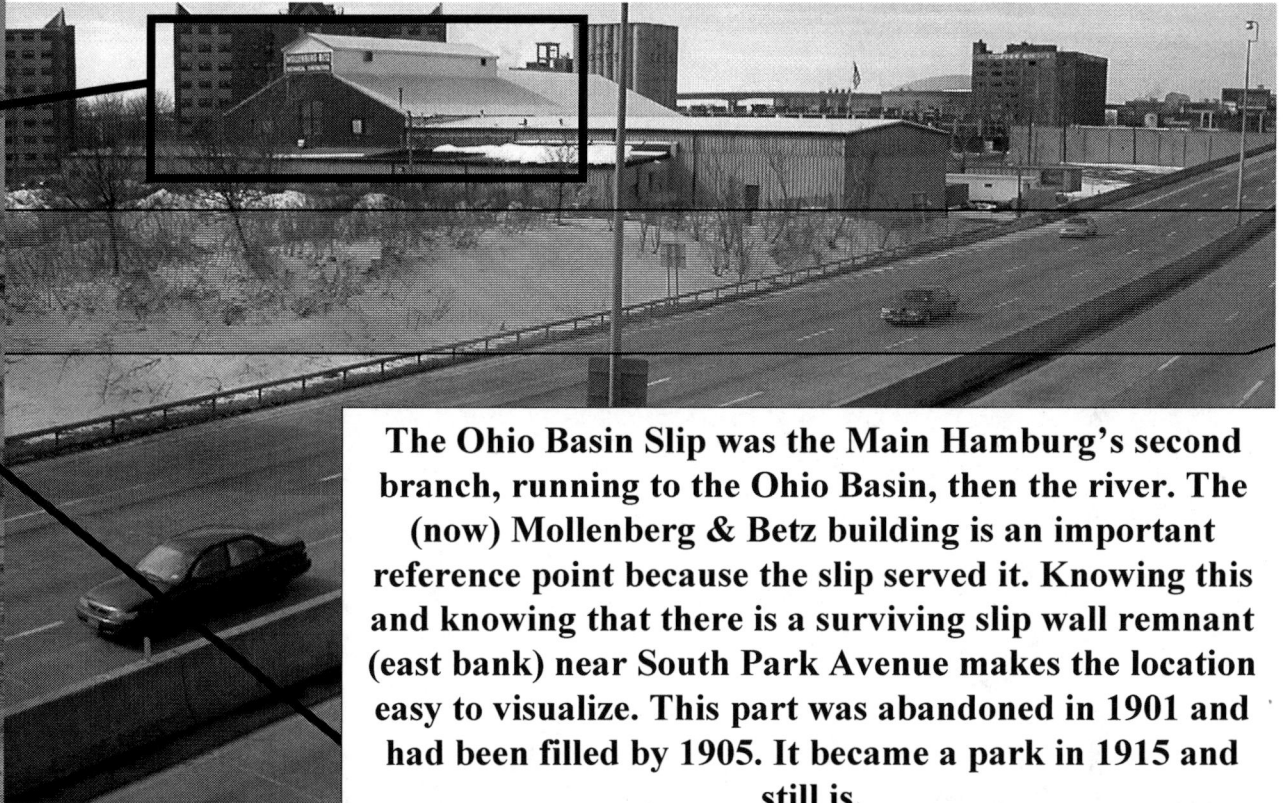

The Ohio Basin Slip was the Main Hamburg's second branch, running to the Ohio Basin, then the river. The (now) Mollenberg & Betz building is an important reference point because the slip served it. Knowing this and knowing that there is a surviving slip wall remnant (east bank) near South Park Avenue makes the location easy to visualize. This part was abandoned in 1901 and had been filled by 1905. It became a park in 1915 and still is.

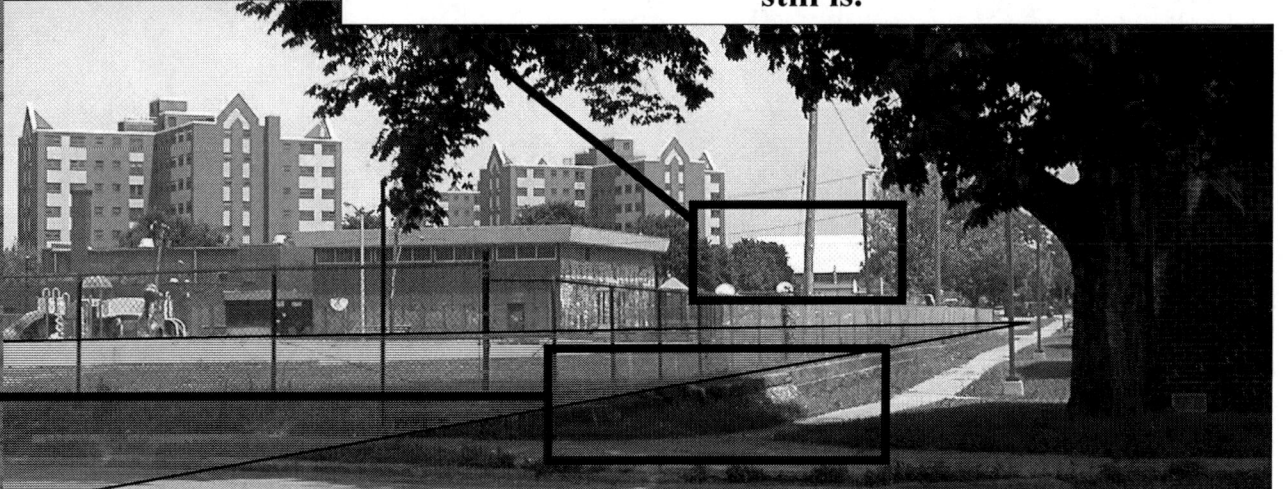

Ohio Basin Slip *page 2*

The 1894 map shows a rail bridge over the slip at Scott Street. Bridge abutments are massive and so tend not to be removed. At this point Scott Street has a ditch but no sidewalk. Both the rail bridge abutment and the (perpendicular) slip wall are visible.

RAIL BRIDGE

SLIP WALL

Scott Street

The park fence pier was probably mounted on top of the bottom half of the slip wall, with this stubborn piece of top section surviving. It has a groove on it which could be from towlines. The slip continued across Elk Street (now South Park Avenue), under the rail embankment bridge and on to the Basin.

Slip Wall

SOUTH PARK AVE

LOUISIANA ST

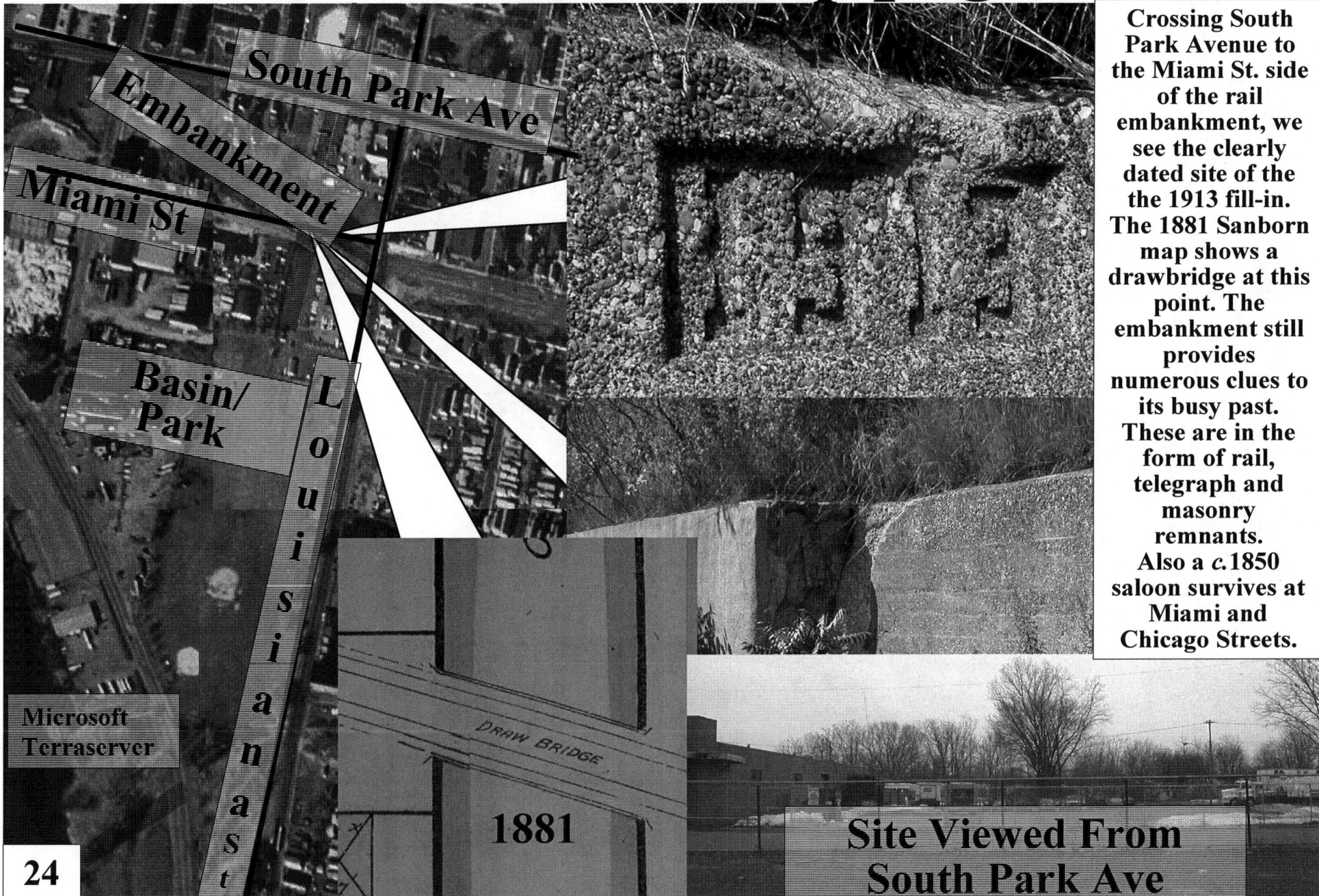

South Park Ave

Embankment

Miami St

Basin/ Park

Louisiana St

DRAW BRIDGE

1881

Site Viewed From South Park Ave

Crossing South Park Avenue to the Miami St. side of the rail embankment, we see the clearly dated site of the the 1913 fill-in. The 1881 Sanborn map shows a drawbridge at this point. The embankment still provides numerous clues to its busy past. These are in the form of rail, telegraph and masonry remnants. Also a *c.*1850 saloon survives at Miami and Chicago Streets.

24

Ohio Basin *in 1935 & 2004*

Filled in the early 1950s and now Conway Park. Both of these pictures were taken from Louisiana Street, near O'Connell Street. Note the locations of the basin wall at lower left and the Great Northern Elevator at upper right.

Western New York Heritage

McLA

MCL

25

Ohio Basin *in 1850, 1995 & 2004*

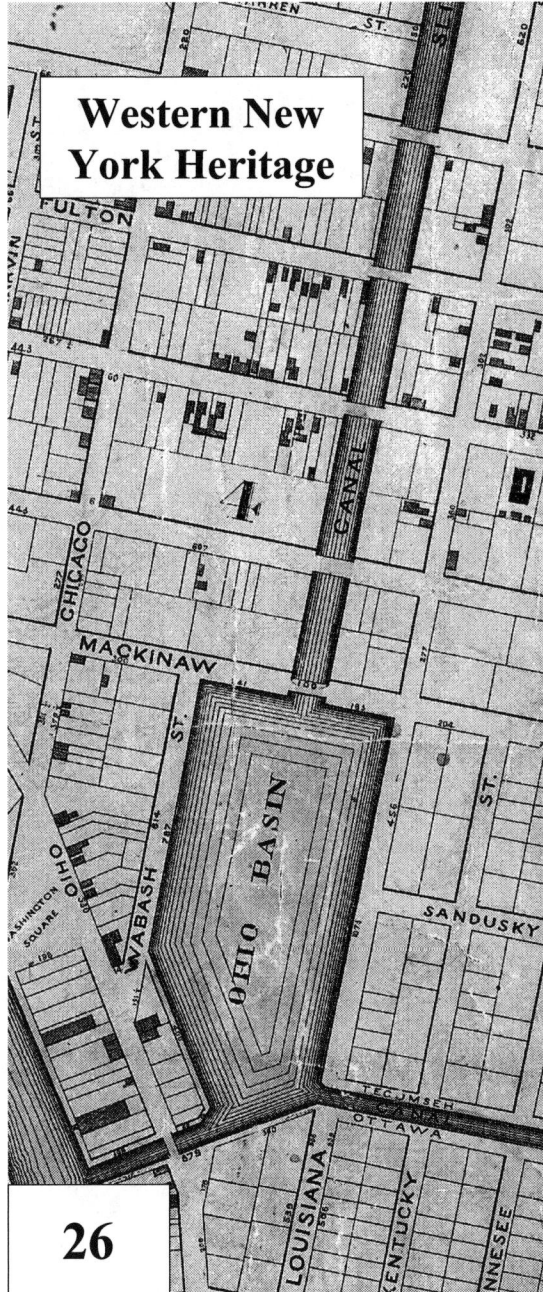

Western New York Heritage

Microsoft Terraserver.com

Filled in, but definitely still there .

From left: 1850 Map, 1995 satellite photograph and cross section visible in 2004 at the entry slip near the Buffalo River.

Tecumseh Ottawa Slip (Republic St.)

A good reason for bad drainage.
Another of the system's extremities in this area, though a short lived one. The map at left is from 1850; by 1872 this slip had been filled and converted to railroad use. Tecumseh Street, the slip and Ottawa Street have been replaced by the railroad tracks and Republic Street. The Ohio Basin is now Conway Park. The proposed canal at bottom left of the map appears never to have been built.
Photo background: Great Northern Elevator.

Western New York Heritage

27

Ohio Entry Slip

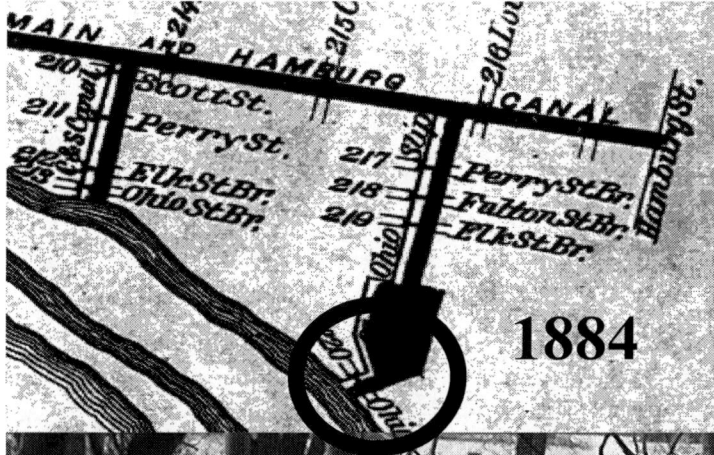

1884

While much attention has been focused on the Commercial Slip, the Ohio Entry Slip has been there all along. The Ohio Basin was filled (with debris from Frank Lloyd Wright's Larkin Administration Building) in the early 1950s and is now the site of Conway Park. The slip running from it to the Buffalo River was filled in as far as Ohio Street – but not beyond. Alternately known as Dead Creek, this slip is the farthest point (from Albany) ever reached by the Erie Canal system. Adjacent is a small park with a canoe launch, picnic tables and a parking area.

Ohio Entry Slip at Buffalo River

This overlooked area is remarkable archeologically and aesthetically. Above, two more photographs of the Ohio Entry Slip. The stone pier at left is viewed from the river, near the slip.

City Ship Canal

WATSON
ELEVATOR.

In June of 2004 the self-unloader Joseph H. Frantz delivers wheat to the General Mills plant, close to the present mouth of the City Ship Canal. The canal was dug in 1850 and from the 1860s until 1907 its mouth was the site of the Watson Elevator. The Watson burned down in that year and in 1913 the land it had stood on was removed to enable ships to turn. The 1897 Great Northern Elevator is located further down the east bank. The west bank never was as heavily industrialized as its neighbor, though the recreational boating business appears healthy.

Several slips ran from the ship canal, through the peninsula, to the Buffalo River. Though all are now filled, their locations are easy to spot.

LeHigh Valley Canal and Basins

from *The Grain Elevators: Buffalo's Lost Industry* by Aaron T. Heverin
<http://www.buffalohistoryworks.com/grain/map/map.htm>

MARSH

RIVER

LEHIGH VALLEY BASINS

BASIN

1946 FILL-IN

LEHIGH VALLEY CANAL

CITY SHIP CANAL

From 1882 to 1946 the City Ship Canal continued on to the LeHigh Valley transfer facility, today's Tifft Nature Preserve. The Makowski Visitor Center's porch is in line with the former center basin. There are excellent then & now displays inside, and you can find the occasional rail remnant on the preserve's trails. The east basin's south leg (top right), and the route of the LeHigh Valley Canal are still clearly visible. The LeHigh Valley Company's original plan called for another three basins on the east of the site (today's marsh area), which were not built.

In 1959 Union Ship Canal *In 2004*

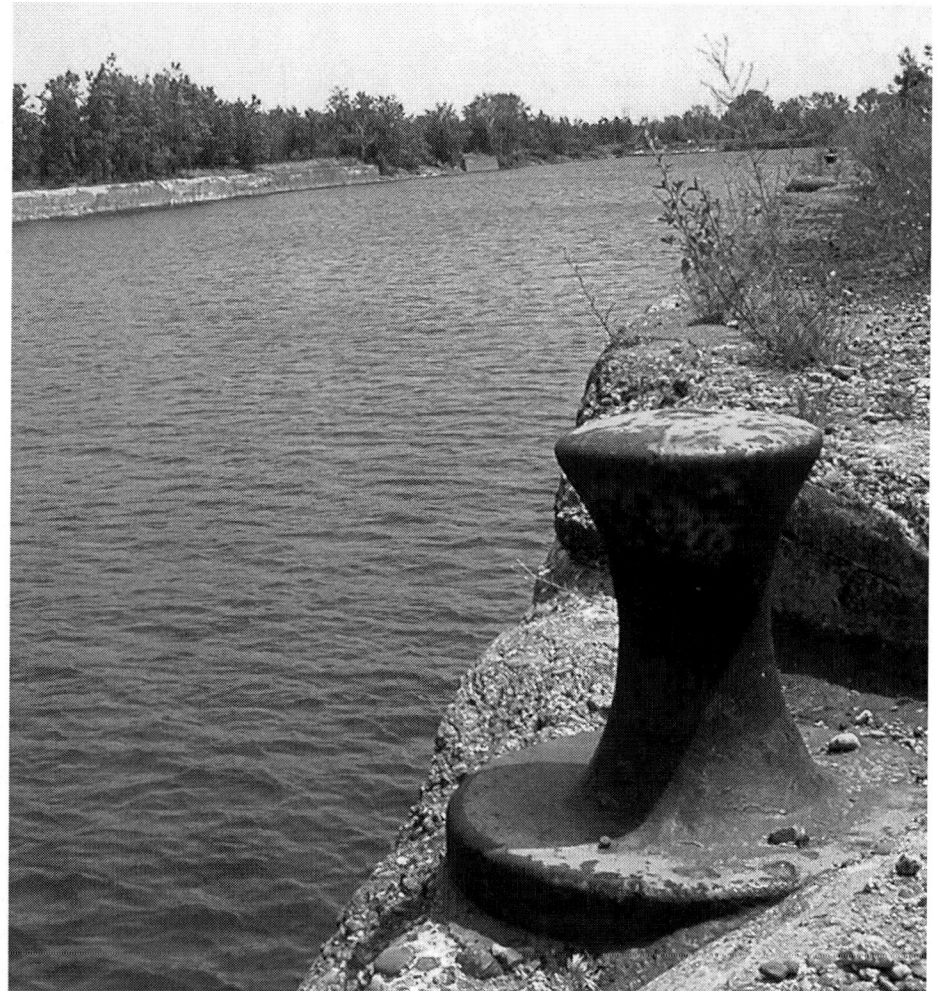

Buffalo & Erie County Historical Society

The Union Ship Canal opened as the Goodyear Slip, in 1905. The aerial shot predates the Father Baker bridge (similar to downtown Buffalo's Skyway), which stood from 1960 until its demolition in 1989. Hanna Furnace had ceased iron making operations in 1982, the end of ore carrier traffic making the high bridge obsolete. The new lower bridge allows access to recreational craft, but in 2004 there is little interest in the area. The pending redevelopment may change this. The nearby Bethlehem Slip, inside the Lackawanna steel plant, has a similar history.

Buffalo Hydraulic Canal

1850 map of Buffalo's Hydraulic Loop, superimposed on a modern map of the area. Note how closely Seymour Street corresponds to the hydraulic route: in 1850 the location consisted of North Canal Street, the Hydraulic Canal, and South Canal Street. Roseville Street (named Porter in the 19th century) is also a good reference point. In the years after the Civil War, industrial waterwheels began to be replaced by steam engines. The Hydraulics fell into disuse, and the Main Hamburg canal began to stagnate.   Bottom Right: The hump in the tunnel under the Larkin building shows the location of the former millrace.

SWAN

SENECA

SEYMOUR

SENECA

HYDRAULIC ST

EXCHANGE

HAMBURG

MH CANAL

ROSEVILLE

Baltic Pl

Seymour St

Carroll St

Griffin St

Van Rensselaer St

Exchange St

Hamburg St

Seneca St

Exchange St

LITTLE BUFFALO

←I-190↓

Western New York Heritage 1850 map over Yahoo Inc. 2005 map.

33

Ebenezer Hydraulic System

Remains of Dam

Mill Race

UNION RD

RACE ST

Although this system was not located within our City of Buffalo target area, its site is accessible and visible. (*Mill*)Race Street is the continuation of Indian Church Road as it crosses Union Road in West Seneca. The remains are contained within the Burchfield Park, which would appear to ensure their preservation. The park is also the site of the Middle Ebenezer Cemetery, the Charles Burchfield Art Center and a children's playground. Excellent maps and signs describe the brief (1840s-1860s) but industrious stay of the Ebenezer Society.

CREDITS

1872, 1881 and 1884 maps, Buffalo and Erie County Public Library, Special Collections Room, Central Branch

1850 map, Western New York Heritage Press, Inc., 2001

1860 American Canal Map, from Brinkley, Alan. *American History A Survey*. McGraw-Hill, 1995

2005 maps, Yahoo! Inc.

Schwab quote from The Mayors of Buffalo. Rizzo, Michael. 2001
<http://www.buffalonian.com/history/industry/mayors/Schwab.htmBuffalonian.com>

Bird's Eye View of the City of Buffalo, NY on display at the Buffalo & Erie County Historical Society
Museum, photographed by Chuck LaChiusa

1904 view of Clark & Skinner Canal from Buffalo Scrapbook, Main Library

1935 Ohio Basin view from *Waterview Guide to Buffalo Harbor*: Glaser, Messmer & Redding, Pub. LLMHC
and WNY Heritage Institute, Buffalo, 1989

Satellite view of Ohio Basin : Microsoft Terraserver <terraserver-usa.com>

LeHigh Valley detail from <http://www.buffalohistoryworks.com/
grain/map/map.htm>

West Frieze, Buffalo City Hall

Bibliography

Baxter, Henry and Heyl, Erik. *Maps Buffalo Harbor*. Buffalo, 1965

Garrity, Richard. *Canal Boatman*. Syracuse, 1977

Tielman, Timothy. *Buffalo's Waterfront*. Buffalo, 1990

Vogel, Michael N., Edward J. Patton and Paul F. Redding. *America's Crossroads: Buffalo's Canal Street/Dante Place*. Buffalo, 1993.

Notes of Thanks

Lower Lakes Marine Historical Society Museum, 66 Erie St., Buffalo and Dan Reilly, Larkin at Exchange

It Was Around Here Somewhere....

Steve Corbett lives and works in Buffalo. When the Commercial Slip excavations began,
he started to wonder about the canals that ran to and from that historic location.
He found that while some are filled or buried, some simply hide in plain sight.
We hope this book will provide both good reading and interesting field trips.